The Mindful Driver

Overcoming Anxiety, Fear and Phobia of Driving Using Mindfulness Techniques

The Mindful Driver

Overcoming Anxiety, Fear and Phobia of Driving Using Mindfulness Techniques

Foreword

Do you feel anxious when you think about driving?

Do your palms sweat as you grip the wheel?

Do images of crashes and collisions flash through your mind even as you drive down a deserted road?

Driving anxiety is so more common than you might think and the best news is that with the right information, time and commitment, it is completely treatable. Driving **can** be easier, less anxiety provoking and even enjoyable. In this book you will receive guidance and information in relation to techniques that you can utilize in order to help reduce your anxiety – specifically your driving anxiety. Becoming confident and comfortable behind the wheel definitely isn't easy, especially when your brain is so used to reacting and responding in a particular way. But with time and training you will slowly learn to retrain your brain and to take control of the overwhelming anxieties that are currently restricting you. It's hard, but believe me you can do it. I avoided addressing my driving fears for over 9 years -- it took weeks to feel like a confident, mindful driver again.

Acknowledgements

I would like to extend my sincerest thanks to my family for helping me through my own driving anxiety and for encouraging me to share my experience with others in writing this book.

Table of Contents

Introduction

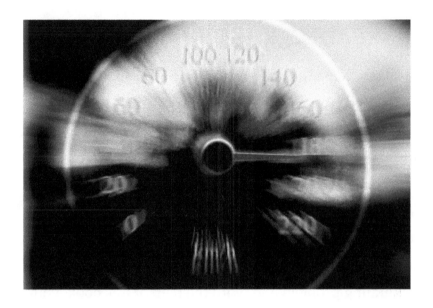

Driving phobia, or driving anxiety, is much more common than you might think. Countless individuals remain confined in their homes, feeling trapped and experiencing a sense of overwhelming dread at the thought of sitting behind the wheel, social commitments are cancelled, and regular routines disrupted - all due to fear of driving. If you suffer from driving anxiety, then you are not alone. More importantly the symptoms that you experience as a result of this anxiety can be managed successfully, you have the ability to take control of your fear and manage your anxieties. This isn't easy and it takes time and commitment,

Introduction

however through continued practice utilizing mindfulness and relaxation techniques you can increase your confidence and comfort on the road so you will be able to drive without feeling completely overwhelmed.

This book will introduce you to the basics about driving anxiety including its causes and the different types of driving anxiety. You will also receive helpful and practical tips for utilizing mindfulness techniques to overcome your driving fears. By the time you finish this book you will not only have a greater understanding of your driving anxiety, but you will also be equipped with the tools you need to turn your life around. Driving anxiety does not need to a debilitating problem and, with the help of this book, you may be able to completely reverse and eliminate your own driving anxiety.

Chapter One: About Driving Anxiety

Driving anxiety, or fear of driving, is more common than you might think. You are not the only one. Countless individuals experience fear, nervousness, or outright panic when it comes to the thought of driving a car. Fortunately, there are ways to conquer your fears and to improve your confidence as a driver. In this chapter you will learn the basics about driving anxiety including the symptoms, causes, and the different types. You will also learn about anxiety in general including information about its effects on both your brain and body.

1.) What is Driving Anxiety and Why Do I Have It?

Driving anxiety is also known as driving phobia or simply "fear of driving" and it is a fairly common condition. This condition often renders people unable to drive at all due to persistent fear or symptoms of anxiety related to driving. It is estimated that between 5% and 10% of all drivers suffer from some form of driving anxiety throughout their lives and, in many cases, driving anxiety can have a severe negative impact on your quality of life.

Think about this – if you are afraid to drive a car, you may have to find an alternative method of transportation. In some cases you might be able to utilize public transportation methods like buses, trains, and taxis – you may even be able to walk or ride your bike to certain locations. If you live in a rural area, however, or if your city doesn't offer much public transportation, you could end up being stuck at home without a way to get around. Relying on friends or family members for rides might work for a little while but you cannot always expect someone else to drop what they are doing to give you a ride.

Driving anxiety can have a very real impact on your quality of life - not just in limiting your ability to go the places you need to go. Many people with driving anxiety will avoid situations that require them to drive at all costs. For example, one might pass over a job opportunity if it requires driving to the office. Having a fear of driving my limit your opportunities to spend time with friends and family or to engage in other activities you enjoy. In some extreme cases, individuals with driving anxiety are not just anxious about driving a car themselves but they are fearful about even being in a car with another driver.

a.) Symptoms of Driving Anxiety

Driving anxiety comes in different forms and each person reacts to it differently. You will learn specifics about the four types of driving anxiety in the next section but, for now, we will review some of the most common symptoms associated with driving anxiety:

- Trembling
- Accelerated pulse
- Sweating
- Loss of sense of reality
- Thoughts of losing control
- Extreme fear or panic
- Disorientation or confusion
- Dry mouth
- Dizziness or shortness of breath

Driving anxiety can be so severe that people can actually experience a panic attack when they are driving or when faced with the idea of driving. According to the Anxiety and Depression Association of America (AADA), a panic attack (or anxiety attack) is *"the abrupt onset of intense fear or discomfort that reaches a peak within minutes and includes at least four of the following symptoms:"*

- Pounding heart, palpitations, accelerated heartrate
- Trembling or shaking
- Sweating
- Shortness of breath
- Sensation of smothering/choking
- Chest pain or discomfort
- Abdominal distress or nausea
- Feeling lightheaded, dizzy, or faint
- Chills or sensation of heat
- Numbness or tingling sensations
- Feelings of unreality, depersonalization
- Fear of losing control
- Fear of dying

Not everyone who experiences driving anxiety will have a full-blown panic attack when operating a vehicle or when faced with the idea of driving. For many people, the symptoms of driving anxiety develop over time, becoming more severe over a period of weeks, months, or years. In many cases, the onset of driving anxiety is linked to a traumatic experience and it may be coupled with post-traumatic stress disorder.

b) Causes of Driving Anxiety

Each person who suffers from driving anxiety has their own unique set of symptoms - the condition may be caused by something specific or it may be related to a general fear of driving. There are three main causes for driving anxiety:

1. **Fear of traffic accidents**
2. **Specific phobia related to driving**
3. **An extension of agoraphobia**

Fear of Traffic Accidents.

The most common cause of driving anxiety is linked to a fear of having an accident. In many cases, driving anxiety develops after the person has experienced an accident and it may be linked to post-traumatic stress disorder (PTSD). Typically, this type of driving anxiety is triggered when the person finds themselves in a similar situation as the accident. For example, if the accident occurred at night, the person might experience driving anxiety only when driving at night. It is also possible for an accident to trigger general driving anxiety, however.

Specific Phobia

The second most common cause of driving anxiety is a specific phobia. A phobia is defined as, *"an extreme or irrational fear of or aversion to something"* – in this case, driving. Driving a car does involve some danger as well as the possibility of a collision – both of these fears are completely normal in a rational person. When this fear becomes intense or induces panic, however, it is classified as a phobia – the level of anxiety or fear does not rationally reflect the actual level of danger.

Extension of Agoraphobia

The third most common cause of driving anxiety is related to agoraphobia. Agoraphobia is defined as, *"an extreme or irrational fear of crowded spaces or enclosed public places"*. It may also be related to fear of having a panic attack when in a public place. Cases of driving anxiety that are linked to agoraphobia are often linked to a fear of being away from home – when a person with agoraphobia drives, they may become anxious about traveling a large distance away from home or about having a panic attack while driving.

2) Types of Driving Anxiety

Now that you have a better understanding of what driving anxiety is and what symptoms it causes you will be better equipped to understand the different types of driving anxiety. There are four main types of driving anxiety, several of which are closely linked to the three causes of driving anxiety discussed in the previous section. The four main types of driving anxiety are:

1. **Driving anxiety caused by panic attacks in association with agoraphobia.**

2. Driving anxiety resulting from a traumatic accident/PTSD.
3. Driving anxiety due to a high risk assessment/fear of crashing.
4. Driving anxiety resulting from a sense of incompetency.

Driving Anxiety Caused by Panic Attacks/Agoraphobia

As you have already learned, agoraphobia is the fear of crowded/public spaces as well as the fear of having a panic attack in a crowded or public area – it is also sometimes described as a fear of being in a public place where one cannot easily get help in the event of an accident or panic attack. Driving anxiety caused by agoraphobia is often related to one's fear of leaving the house and it can be triggered by stressful or fear-inducing situations like driving.

According to a recent survey, more than 40% of people with agoraphobia considered driving on a highway to be a panic attack-inducing event. In this type of driving anxiety, the fear is two-fold. Not only is it related to fear of having a panic attack while driving but there is also the fear of losing control of the vehicle, causing a crash or collision.

Sometimes when people experience a panic attack they have feelings of losing control or losing consciousness – many agoraphobics with driving anxiety fear that these things will happen while they are behind the wheel.

Driving Anxiety Resulting from a Traumatic Accident

Many drivers who experience a serious accident report symptoms of post-traumatic stress disorder. Even those who do not suffer from PTSD following an accident may still experience feelings of uneasiness or anxiety while driving. This is simply because they have already experienced an accident and they fear that it may happen again. In extreme cases, the individual may actually experience flashbacks to the accident while driving – these flashbacks can cause the individual to re-live the traumatic experience again and again.

This type of driving anxiety can occur in individuals who never had a problem driving previous to the accident. After experiencing driving-related trauma, however, they may become fearful of driving to the point that they refuse to get behind the wheel again. The level of driving anxiety resulting from a traumatic accident varies from one individual to another. In some people it may only produce fear of certain situations such as driving on a highway or driving at night. In others, however, it can become so severe that the individual avoids driving altogether.

Driving Anxiety Due to High Risk Assessment

Even people who have not experienced a driving accident can be fearful of the potential risks involved with driving. In some cases these fears may be borne of second-hand experience, such as a friend or family member getting in a serious accident. In other cases it may be based on news stories or a general feeling that the world is a scary and dangerous place. People who have a fear of driving like this often pay special attention to news reports and stories involving accidents to justify their fears, using it as evidence against driving. Individuals with this type of driving anxiety are often resistant to arguments to counter-balance this.

Driving Anxiety Resulting from a Sense of Incompetency

The fourth type of driving anxiety is related to a sense of incompetency. Individuals who have experienced minor accidents in the past, who have failed a driving test, or those who have had their driving criticized by others often develop feelings of incompetency surrounding their driving skills and may feel anxious while driving as a result. Individuals with this type of driving anxiety may still drive but they might be less confident in their abilities than they used to be or they might avoid certain situations.

3) Understanding Anxiety – How it Affects Your Body and Brain

Now that you understand the basics of driving anxiety including the different types you will be better able to understand what anxiety is in general and how it affects your brain. Anxiety is more than just nervousness or discomfort – it can affect the way you feel, the way you think, and how you act. In short, anxiety can dominate your whole being and can be a real struggle to deal with day to day.

According to Medical News Today, anxiety is often triggered by stress and some people are more prone to developing anxiety than others. It is normal to experience a little bit of anxiety in certain situations but, for some people, anxiety becomes severe and it may even be present in the absent of any real threat or danger. In cases like this, anxiety can interfere with your life, your job, your relationships, and even your way of thinking. Anxiety is a very real problem for some people and it can be difficult to live with and deal with.

In order to help you deal with your driving anxiety, you may want to think about these key facts:

- **Anxiety is completely normal**. Everyone experiences a little anxiety now and again, so do not feel guilty if you suffer from an anxiety problem.

- **Anxiety serves a purpose**. Anxiety exists to help you prepare for real danger or to do your best in certain situations. For example, feeling anxious in the days leading up to a big presentation at work may cause you to work harder and to fully prepare yourself. Anxiety is also what causes your "fight or flight" response – for example, it is what allows you to jump out of the path of a speeding vehicle coming your way.

- **Anxiety cannot hurt you**. Though anxiety may cause you discomfort in the form of various physical symptoms, it is not physically dangerous or harmful. The symptoms you experience related to anxiety are part of your body's "fight or flight response" – they are designed to protect you.

- **Anxiety is temporary**. When you are experiencing anxiety it may feel like it will last forever, but it is only temporary. In this book you will learn many techniques to help you reduce your anxiety.

- **Anxiety problems are very common**. Anxiety is something that everyone experiences and anxiety problems are more common than you might think. If you suffer from an anxiety condition, you are not alone.

- Anxiety affects each person differently in terms of what situations or actions trigger your anxiety. When it comes to your body's physical response, however, many people experience anxiety in the same ways such as:

- Rapid heartbeat and fast breathing

- Nausea or upset stomach
- Tightness or pain in the chest
- Feeling dizzy or lightheaded
- Numbness or tingling
- Fuzzy vision, feelings of unreality

Rapid Heartbeat/Breathing

When your body is preparing itself for potential action (your "fight or flight response"), it starts to pump more blood and oxygen to your essential organs and major muscle groups. Increased blood and oxygen will give you the energy and power you need to escape a dangerous situation.

Nausea or Upset Stomach

When your body senses danger, it shuts down unessential systems and processes in favor of those that are needed to ensure survival. Digestion is a process that is not needed in times of danger, so your body funnels blood and oxygen away from the digestive system toward more essential muscles and organs – this can lead to feelings of nausea or stomach upset.

Tightness/Pain in Chest

In a fight or flight response your muscles may tighten in preparation for sudden movement – you will also start to breathe more heavily. Both of these things may contribute to tightness or pain in the chest.

Feeling Dizzy/Lightheaded

In preparation for fight or flight, your body starts to pump more oxygen and blood to your essential organs and major muscle groups – you will also start to breathe more quickly. In some cases, hyperventilation may occur which could make you feel dizzy or lightheaded. It may also be the case that most of your blood and oxygen starts flowing to the arms and legs, meaning there is less blood and oxygen flowing to your brain which could also cause these feelings.

Numbness or Tingling

Fast or heavy breathing can cause hyperventilation which may also lead to feelings of numbness or tingling in your extremities. These feelings may also be the result of hairs standing up on your body as part of your body's "fight or flight" response – this increases your sensitivity to touch and movement. As more blood flows to your major muscle groups and essential organs, there may be less of it in your fingers and toes which also contributes to feelings of numbness/tingling.

Not only does anxiety trigger certain physical responses in your body, but it has an effect on your brain as well. As you've already learned, anxiety invokes a certain "fight or flight" response in your body and it may cause your body to react in a similar way that stress does. When you feel stress, your body produces stress hormones like cortisol which help to enhance your reflexes and speed while increasing your heartrate and circulation in preparation for fight or flight. Stress can occur in combination with a variety of emotions not limited to fear – these emotions may also include happiness, sadness, anger or excitement.

Anxiety, on the other hand, is always associated with feelings of fear, dread or apprehension. In many cases, anxiety is forged by experience. For example, if you come from an abusive home where yelling is a common occurrence, your brain may become wired for anxiety – you may find yourself constantly on the lookout for potentially dangerous situations. In other cases, however, anxiety may be the result of a chemical imbalance in your brain. If your brain doesn't produce the right amount of mood-controlling neurotransmitters, you may be pre-disposed to certain anxiety disorders. The good news is that most anxiety disorders are treatable.

Neurotransmitters are a type of chemical that send messages to your brain dictating how you feel, think, and act in certain situations. Some of the neurotransmitters that have been specifically linked to anxiety include serotonin, GABA, and norepinephrine. Having too much or too little of any of these hormones can affect your anxiety levels. Unfortunately, there is still a great deal to be learned about brain chemistry, particularly neurotransmitter production. It is difficult to distinguish between cases where anxiety is the result of life experience or if it is due to genetics.

There are two different components of any anxiety disorder – the mental component and the physical component. The physical component is related to those symptoms we have already covered – things like lightheadedness, rapid heartbeat, sweating, etc. The mental component involves your nervous thoughts and worries related to your anxiety. Certain hormones have specific effects on the brain and body as well.

For example, adrenaline is one of the most common causes for anxiety symptoms – your body releases this hormone when your "fight or flight" system is activated. Adrenaline is the hormone that causes your heart to beat faster, your breathing to increase, and your muscles to become tense. Long-term or chronic stress may alter your body's ability to control adrenaline production which may lead to anxiety symptoms. Thyroid hormone is also closely related to anxiety symptoms. This hormone helps to regulate production of neurotransmitters including norepinephrine, serotonin, and Gamma-aminobutryic acid (GABA). For this reason, thyroid problems may also increase your risk for certain anxiety disorders.

Panic attacks also play a key role in brain activity. Research has shown that individuals who suffer from panic attacks often exhibit an overactive amygdala. The amygdala is the part of the brain that is plays a primary role in processing memory, in making decisions, and in processing emotions. This is the part of the brain that signals to the rest of your brain when a threat is imminent – it causes the activation of your fight or flight response. Emotional memories stored in the amygdala may be related to anxiety disorders caused by specific fears or phobias such as spiders, dogs, or driving.

Unfortunately, it is estimated that only about one third of individuals suffering from an anxiety disorder ever receive treatment. Many of those who suffer from anxiety suffer in silence. There is still a great deal of stigma against mental disorders like anxiety and depression which discourages some people from seeking the treatment they need. Even those who do seek treatment for anxiety do so in the form of pharmaceutical drugs which may help relieve the symptoms of anxiety but they generally do not deal with the underlying problem.

One of the most effective treatments for anxiety is psychotherapy including mindfulness techniques, breathing exercises, and Emotional Freedom Techniques (EFTs).

Chapter Two: Mindfulness and Anxiety

According to Psychology Today, mindfulness is, "a state of active, open attention on the present". Being mindful involves observing your thoughts and emotions objectively, without judging, and being actively involved in the moment. Mindfulness techniques are not only useful in reducing your stress, but it can also be very helpful in reducing your driving anxiety. In this chapter you will learn the basics about mindfulness including, how it helps with anxiety, and how to get started.

1.) What is Mindfulness?

Many people who suffer from anxiety feel guilty about themselves and often engage in negative self-talk. When they experience feelings of anxiety, those feelings are magnified by guilt and by feelings of incompetence or low self-esteem.

Mindfulness involves cultivating an awareness of your thoughts and feelings, becoming more "mindful" of them, without being judgmental. Thoughts and emotions are not labeled as "good" or "bad" – they are what they are and that's all there is to it.

The practice of mindfulness has its roots in Buddhist meditation; however it is rapidly becoming popular in the secular world. There are thousands of research studies which have documented the mental and physical health benefits of mindfulness techniques in general, as well as those connected to stress reduction and the treatment of various anxiety disorders. Practicing mindfulness for even a few weeks can produce some very real benefits, some of which are listed below:

- A research study has shown that practicing mindfulness techniques for just 8 weeks can boost your immune system's defenses against illness and infection.

- Practicing mindfulness techniques will increase positive emotions while reducing stress and negative emotions – it may even be as effective as antidepressant medications in treating depression.

- Mindfulness techniques, when practiced regularly, can actually change your brain – it increases the density of gray matter in areas linked to emotion regulation, memory, and learning.

- Practicing mindfulness techniques may help you to tune out distractions so you can improve your focus and memory.

- Mindfulness not only helps you to feel better about yourself but it may also increase feelings of empathy, compassion, and altruism – it also boosts feelings of self-compassion.

- When you practice mindfulness you may improve your relationship with your partner – it is also good for parents and parents to-be, helping to reduce stressand anxiety.

- Mindfulness techniques can be applied to eating habits, helping you to achieve "mindful eating" to lose weight and fight obesity.

- When used in schools, mindfulness can reduce aggression and behavioral problems among students and it may increase their ability to pay attention.

There are several ways to go about practicing mindfulness techniques and certain practices are beneficial for specific types of stress and anxiety. In the next section you will learn about how mindfulness can be beneficial for general anxiety.

2) How can Mindfulness Help with Anxiety?

While many mindfulness techniques are rooted in meditation, that is not the only option. Mindfulness is about increasing your awareness of your own thoughts and emotions – it is also about living in the moment. Some of the key components of mindfulness techniques are:

- Learning to pay attention to your breathing – this is especially important when you are experiencing anxiety symptoms.

- Notice what you are sensing in the moment – pay attention to sights, sounds, and smells in your surroundings.

- Recognize your thoughts and emotions – realize that they are temporary and that they do not define you.

- Become attuned to the physical sensations of your body.

One of the main benefits of mindfulness exercises for anxiety is its ability to help you process your emotions. The question, "How are you feeling?" plays a key role in mindfulness for anxiety and it can help you to tame your emotions, fostering positive emotions and letting go of negative emotions. For many people, anxiety is a cycle that feeds on your fear and insecurities – with mindfulness exercises you can recognize and deal with those fears and insecurities to tame your anxiety.

On the following pages you will find descriptions of several mindfulness techniques you can use to reduce your anxiety.

a.) Naming Your Fear

When you start to feel the symptoms of anxiety – increased heartrate, fast breathing, chest tightening – allow an imaginary alarm bell to sound in your head. Learning to recognize your anxiety is the first step to dealing with it. Stop what you are doing and take three deep, slow breaths. It may help you to place one hand on your heart to feel your heartrate and another on your belly, encouraging you to breathe deeply. Take another few breaths, deep and slow, until your heartrate starts to normalize.

As you breathe, allow yourself to acknowledge your fear – tell yourself, "I am afraid and it is okay." Take a few moments to recognize what is causing your anxiety and name your fear – "I am feeling anxious because ___." Naming your fear automatically creates distance which will help to lessen your emotional reaction. Once you have named your fear and have started to calm down, tell yourself these positive phrases:

"I see the source of my fear. I am safe and free from my fear. I am happy and at ease."

b) Leaning in to Your Fear

When you feel anxious or fearful, it can be tempting to push it away and to not deal with it. Part of mindfulness, however, is acknowledging your fear and dealing with it directly. When you start to experience negative thoughts and emotions, do not treat them as a threat – acknowledge them but do not allow them to take power over you. Identify each individual fear and let it go – breathe deeply, allowing your negative emotions to flow out of your body with each breath. You may also repeat the phrases from the previous exercise as you breathe away each individual fear or negative thought/emotion.

These simple exercises are powerful tools for dealing with any kind of anxiety or fear that you might experience. As simple as they are, these kind of exercise are the key to mindfulness – you must acknowledge your thoughts and emotions, viewing them objectively, and must not allow them to take control over you. In the next section you will learn about some of the specific benefits of mindfulness techniques for driving anxiety.

3.) Mindfulness for Driving Anxiety

For many people, driving anxiety is closely related to a fear of losing control. If you suffer from panic attacks, you may feel trapped behind the wheel of a car, plagued with thoughts of what would happen if you were to experience a panic attack while driving. Sometimes people who experience panic attacks feel like they are about to lose control – when driving a car, they might worry about suddenly swerving into oncoming traffic or driving through a guardrail and over a cliff. Mindfulness activities are about acknowledging and taming not only your fears, but your thoughts and emotions as well. By properly applying mindfulness techniques you can reduce your driving anxiety significantly.

In the last section you learned the basics about applying mindfulness activities to anxiety in general, but in this section you will learn more specifically how mindfulness can be applied to driving anxiety. Mindfulness activities that relate specifically to driving involve increasing your awareness of your surroundings and focusing yourself on the task at hand – operating your vehicle safely. By being mindful you will become a safer and more defensive driver, aware not only of your own intentions but more perceptive to the intentions of others. By driving mindfully you can avoid putting yourself in dangerous situations and, if you find yourself in a potential threatening situation, you will be able to think rationally and logically to get yourself out of it. In the next chapter you will find several mindfulness techniques to help you reduce your driving anxiety.

Chapter Three: Using Mindfulness Techniques to Reduce Pre-Driving Anxiety

For many people who suffer from driving anxiety, the hardest part is simply getting in the car. Your mind is flooded with thoughts of "what if" and you may be paralyzed by fear or uncertainty of what might happen when you turn the key in the ignition and place your foot on the gas. Practicing a few simple breathing exercises and mindfulness techniques before you get into the car can help you to greatly reduce your driving anxiety. You will find step-by-step instructions for several breathing exercises and mindfulness techniques in this chapter.

1.) Breathing Exercises

Breathing is something that we do all day every day without even thinking about it most of the time. When you experience anxiety or a panic attack, however, you maybe come super-focused on your breathing because it may become difficult to breathe or you might be breathing too quickly. Practicing a few simple breathing exercises can help you take back control in anxiety-inducing situations and, if you perform one of these exercises **before driving,** you may find that you feel less anxious on the road.

a.) Mindful Breathing

To practice general mindful breathing techniques, sit comfortably on the ground or in a chair with your hands in your lap and follow these steps:

1. Get comfortable in your chair or on the ground, sitting with your back straight and your hands resting gently in your lap.

2. Start to focus on your breathing, becoming more aware of how breath enters your body through your nose and

mouth, traveling down into your lungs.

3. Notice the temperature of your breath – is it warm or cool? – as it enters your body and notice how the temperature changes as you exhale.

4. Take deep breaths, noticing how the air expands your lungs and fills your belly – breathe at whatever speed is comfortable for you.

5. Become aware of the physical sensations of breathing – do you feel the air passing through your nostrils? Do you feel your stomach expanding?

6. Perform this exercise for five minutes at a time for the first few times then gradually increase the duration, if desired.

7. Try performing this exercise before bed to help improve your quality of sleep – this is particularly beneficial if your anxiety tends to keep you awake at night.

b.) The Bellows Breath/Stimulating Breath Exercise

This particular exercise is aimed toward increasing your alertness by breathing quickly, imitating the motion of a bellows. Follow the steps below:

1. Get comfortable in your chair or on the ground, sitting with your back straight and your hands resting gently in your lap.

2. Keep your mouth gently closed and inhale rapidly through your nose as quickly as possible.

3. Exhale at the same rate as you inhaled, through the nose, keeping your breaths short and quick.

4. As you breathe, focus on keeping your breaths short and feel the effort at the back of your neck as well as in your diaphragm and abdomen.

5. Repeat the process twice for a total of three quick breaths in and out.

6. Take a few normal breaths then repeat the quick in and out for a total of 5 seconds, aiming for three breaths per second.

7. Gradually build your way up to 30 seconds or more of bellows breathing.

8. Perform this exercise to give yourself a natural energy boost instead of reaching for a cup of coffee.

c.) The Relaxing Breath Exercise

This breathing exercise is very calming and it becomes more effective each time you use it. Try to perform this exercise twice per day to reduce your overall stress and anxiety levels. Follow the steps below to perform this exercise properly:

1. Get comfortable in your chair or on the ground, sitting with your back straight and your hands resting gently in your lap.

2. Place the tip of your tongue against the tissue just behind your front teeth, as if you were making a "La" sound.

3. Exhale fully through your mouth (keeping your tongue in position), allowing your breath to make a whooshing sound.

4. Gently close your mouth and inhale silently through your nose over a count of four seconds.

5. Hold your breath for a count of seven seconds – do not allow your body to become tense as you hold it.

6. Exhale slowly through your mouth for a count of eight seconds, allowing your breath to make a loud whooshing sound.

7. Repeat the cycle three more times, beginning with the four-second inhale.

d.) The Breath Counting Exercise

This breathing exercise can be a little challenging at first, but you will get the hang of it after a few repetitions. Follow the steps below for this breathing exercise:

1. Get comfortable in your chair or on the ground, sitting with your back straight and your hands resting gently in your lap.

2. Close your eyes and take a few gentle breaths at whatever pace is comfortable for you – it should be quiet and fairly slow.

3. Inhale comfortably then exhale as you mentally count to one in your head.

4. Inhale again then exhale over a count of two seconds, counting in your head.

5. Repeat the process, increasing the length of your exhale each time up to a count of five – this is one cycle.

6. Begin a new cycle, counting your exhale for a count of one second.

ness Techniques Before Driving

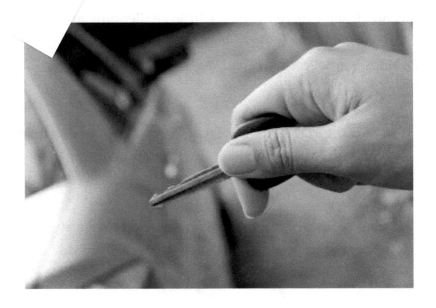

If you suffer from driving anxiety, what you do immediately before driving can be very important. If you do not take time to ground yourself and to center your thoughts, you may be leaving yourself open to a panic attack. If, however, you take a few moments to practice mindfulness techniques and to calm your mind, you may find that your driving anxiety is significantly reduced. To practice mindfulness before driving, follow the steps that are listed on the following pages:

1. Find a quiet room in your house where you will be undisturbed for a few minutes – if you regularly meditate, use the same location.

2. Adjust the lighting in the room so that it is soft and subtle – use a lamp rather than an overhead light and think about covering it with a sheer scarf to reduce the intensity.

3. Feel free to light an aromatherapy candle or incense stick if you think it will help you to relax.

4. Make sure you are wearing loose, comfortable clothing – you may also find it comforting to place a blanket over your legs and a shawl or scarf over your shoulders.

5. Sit in a comfortable chair with your feet flat on the floor and your hands resting gently in your lap – sit slightly forward in the chair so your back isn't against the back of the chair.

6. You may also choose to sit cross-legged on a cushion on the floor – just be sure you will be comfortable enough to remain focused throughout the entire

exercise.

7. Gently sway from side to side for a few moments, focusing on your movements and on your breathing.

8. Take a deep breath, inhaling through your nose to fill your lungs and your diaphragm with air.

9. Exhale for a count of five seconds, expelling as much air from your lungs as possible.

10. Repeat the breaths two more times for a total of three – focus on your inhalations and exhalations as you breathe.

11. Continue to take deep breaths as you visualize your vehicle – imagine yourself approaching the car and getting behind the wheel.

12. Keep breathing as you picture yourself buckling your seatbelt, checking the mirrors, and then turning on the car.

13. Take another three deep breaths in and out then picture yourself pressing gently on the brake, shifting

the car into gear, and moving forward.

14. Continue to breathe calmly as you picture yourself driving toward your destination – remain calm and focus on your breathing.

15. If you begin to feel nervous, place one hand gently over your heart and breathe in slowly through your nose and exhale through your mouth for a count of five.

16. Continue these slow, deep breaths until you feel your heartrate slow back to normal.

17. Picture yourself arriving safely at your destination, continuing your deep breathing, and imagine yourself turning off the car, unbuckling your seatbelt, and exiting the vehicle.

18. Take another three slow, deep breaths in and out before opening your eyes.

19. Performing this exercise before you leave the house will help you to become calmer in anticipation of operating your vehicle. In the next chapter you will

learn some mindfulness techniques to reduce your anxiety while you are actually driving.

Chapter Four: Using Mindfulness to Reduce Anxiety While Driving

The exercises presented in the last chapter are designed to help you reduce your anxiety in general and to help prepare you for operating your vehicle without anxiety. In this chapter you will receive some helpful tips for driving mindfully including a step-by-step guide for mindful driving. These tips will help you to not only drive mindfully, but to reduce your anxiety and to help ensure that you arrive safely at your destination.

1.) Keep Your Fear from Turning into Panic

Fear is a natural defense mechanism that your body has put in place for your own protection. In a dangerous situation, fear motivates you to do what is necessary to get yourself out of the situation. A little bit of fear while you are driving is okay because it will help you to be more alert and more conscious of your surroundings, including other drivers. When you latch on to your fear and feed it, however, it turns into panic and that can become dangerous for you and the other drivers around you. In order to prevent panic attacks while driving, you need to take control of your fear.

Some say that anxiety is the anticipation of fear – that fear may be real and warranted, or it might be irrational and illogical. The key to preventing your fear from turning into severe anxiety or a panic attack is to remain in the moment. Take stock of the other vehicles around you as well as the area through which you are driving. Be Mindful. Think about the marvels of modern technology that enable you to be driving a car in the first place. Keep your breath flowing as steadily as possible as you think about everything but your fear.

If your fear and anxiety starts to worsen, avoid giving in to it and letting it control you. Instead, you need to take control of your fear to get past it. This technique may seem a little counterintuitive at first but after it works for you the first time you will see its merit. Follow these steps to take control of your fear before it turns into panic:

1. If you are able to do so safely, pull your car over to the side of the road or into a parking lot and turn it off.

2. Become aware of your feelings and identify each one – do you feel afraid? Do you feel claustrophobic? What other feelings are you experiencing?

3. Take those feelings and accept them – tell yourself, "I am afraid" or "I am feeling anxious".

4. Next, take note of the physical reactions you are experiencing – tightening of the chest, trembling hands, general jittery feelings.

5. Consciously identify each physical reaction you are having then worsen them yourself – yes, worsen them.

6. If your hands are trembling, put in a conscious effort to make them tremble more –by worsening your

symptoms you are taking control over them.

7. If your body is feeling jittery, make yourself tremble even more – if your chest feels tight, take one hand and press it firmly against your collar bone.

8. If you feel like screaming, let yourself shout something in the car at the top of your lungs. Remember no one can hear you. If you're worried turn up the radio.

9. As you take control of your feelings and physical reactions you will find yourself living in the moment – during a panic attack your mind tends to race ahead,

thinking of every negative possibility that mi
to pass.

10. Once you have come to realize that you are able to control your feelings you will start to relax.

11. Take a few deep breaths with your hand over your heart to steady your breathing before you get back on the road.

This technique is useful if you experience severe anxiety or a panic attack while driving and nothing else works to calm you down. For some people, simple relaxation exercises help to stave off panic while driving. You will find step-by-step instructions for a simple relaxation technique to use while driving listed below:

1. When you start to feel nervous or anxious, take a slow, deep breath in through your nose and exhale through your mouth.

2. Release the tension in your forehead, jaws, and eyes – you may not even realize that you've been clenching

your jaw and wrinkling your forehead.

3. Slightly part your jaws so that there is a gap between your teeth – this will help you to relax your facial muscles and it will help you to become more alert and aware.

4. Gently roll your head to the right a few times then pause and reverse the direction.

5. Roll your shoulders clockwise a few times then pause and reverse, rolling them counter-clockwise a few times.

6. Pull your shoulder blades back toward your spine and hold them there for a few seconds while taking deep breaths.

7. Squeeze the wheel tightly with both of your hands and hold for a second, then relax your grip – repeat this several times to make sure that you aren't gripping the wheel too tightly.

8. Squeeze your buttocks together a few times and relax to release any tension you have been holding there.

9. Take a few more deep breaths and allow yourself to feel relaxed and in control, letting your anxiety dissipate.

This whole exercise should take less than a minute and it is something you can do while waiting at a stop light or by pulling your car off the road. The key to making this exercise successful is to do it when you start to feel the first signs of anxiety – it will help you to avoid a full-blown panic attack. It may help for you to practice this technique a few times at home before you try to use it on the road. Always make sure that you are able to perform the exercise safely if you choose to do it on the road.

2.) Step-by-Step Guide for Mindful Driving

The techniques from the last section are designed to help you stave of fear and panic while driving. In this section we will discuss some mindfulness techniques for driving to help you maintain awareness to keep your anxiety at bay. Below you will find a step-by-step guide for practicing mindful driving:

1. Approach your car with the intention of being mindful as you drive – mindful driving starts before you even

turn on the car.

2. Take note of all of the individual actions involved in starting your car – opening the car door, sitting down, buckling your seatbelt, placing the key in the ignition, turning the key, etc.

3. Become aware of the sensations you are feeling as you perform these tasks – notice the feeling of the door handle against your palm, the feel of the cushioning below your body as you sit, the cold metal of the keys in your hand.

4. Turn on your car and carefully pull out onto the road – as you do, notice the sensation of moving and the feeling of the steering wheel beneath your hands.

5. Expand your awareness to include everything in your surroundings – look for other cars and obstructions before you make your next move.

6. Label each of your behaviors to yourself as you take them and remain intentional about everything you do – as you prepare to change lanes, for example, tell yourself, "I am checking my rearview mirror. I am

checking my side view mirrors. The lane is clear – I am changing lanes."

7. Keep your thoughts focused on your driving and your intentions as you drive – do not let your mind wander and your body go into autopilot.

8. Each time you stop at a stop sign or a red light, use it as an opportunity to refocus yourself, to make sure you are still being mindful.

Continue to drive mindfully until you reach your desired destination. When you do, take a few deep breaths before exiting the vehicle.

As simple as it may be, this mindfulness technique can go a long way in reducing your driving anxiety. For many people, anxiety involves fear of losing control. If you drive mindfully, using the technique described above, you will feel more in control of yourself and your vehicle as you drive. When you feel in control of yourself and your situation, you are less likely to experience anxiety. If you practice this technique each time you drive you will find that driving becomes easier for you and your anxiety becomes less and less of a problem.

Chapter Five: Feeling Safe, Confident and Comfortable on the Road

Overcoming driving anxiety is not about conditioning yourself not to feel fear – it is about increasing your confidence and comfort on the road so that your anxiety does not control you. In this chapter you will receive a number of tips for reducing your anxiety while driving and for increasing your confidence in your driving ability. You will also receive some tips for practicing various techniques to reduce your anxiety in general so you can become a more mindful driver.

1.) Tips for Reducing AnxietyWhile Driving

Practicing mindfulness techniques before and during driving can go a long way to reduce your driving anxiety. There are also a few other things you can do, however, which will complement your mindfulness efforts. In this section you will find a collection of tips to help you further reduce your driving anxiety, especially when you are driving in less than optimal conditions.

Remember It Isn't a Race

When you are driving on the highway you will probably encounter at least one vehicle that is going way over the speed limit, weaving between lanes, and passing at every opportunity. Seeing something like this can rev up your anxiety but do not let it! Remember that you are not in a race – the goal is not to reach your destination as quickly as possible but to reach it safely. Follow speed limit signs and remain in the slow lane whenever possible. Do not let the behavior of unsafe drivers dictate your own driving – do what is comfortable for you. If you find yourself becoming anxious as a result of another driver's behavior, take a few deep breaths and try to concentrate instead on your own mindful driving.

Plan Your Route Before You Leave

For many people who suffer from driving anxiety, it is not just the driving that makes you anxious – other factors play a role as well. For example, you might become anxious if you are unfamiliar with the route you are taking and you might become fearful of getting lost. To help prevent this type of anxiety, take a few moments to study and plan your route before you leave the driveway. Pull up a map on your computer or smartphone before you even get into the car so you know what you first few steps will be – you can even use the Google Maps Street View function to identify landmarks to look for while driving. Then, when you get in the car, plug the destination into your GPS. If you know where you are going and what to look for along the way you will feel more comfortable and confident as you drive.

Practice Putting Yourself in Challenging Situations

When you have anxiety, it can be tempting to avoid any situation that might trigger your anxiety. In reality, the only way you are going to get over your fear is to face it – you may need to put yourself in challenging or anxiety-inducing situations on purpose if you ever hope to conquer your fears. For example, if you get nervous when driving on crowded streets you may want to practice driving during rush hour. If you have a fear of getting lost, drive to a location that you have been to only once or twice and then try to get yourself home without relying on your GPS. The more challenging situations you can think of to test yourself, the more confident a driver you will become.

Try Using a Soothing Sounds CD

For some people, playing music on the radio or by CD can be distracting and a trigger for anxiety. For others, however, having some background noise can help to improve your focus and to soothe your anxiety while driving. Trying to keep up with a conversation with another person in your car can be anxiety-inducing while you are driving, but putting in a CD might be helpful. Try a number of different options to determine what works for you. For some people it might be a CD of soothing nature sounds like whale music or bird songs. For others, it could be loud rock music or something else entirely.

Give Yourself Time

Overcoming driving anxiety is not something that you can do overnight – it takes time. The most important thing you can do for yourself is to be patient and forgiving – do not push yourself too far beyond your limits and do not set unrealistic expectations for yourself. This is not to say that you shouldn't set goals or challenge yourself, but try to take baby steps and make changes over a longer period of time instead of trying to rush yourself into things. Slow progress is lasting progress.

2.) Confidence-Boosting Tips

Becoming a confident driver is not something that just happens – you have to work at it. For many people, driving anxiety is fueled by low self-esteem or a belief that they are incompetent. In order to become a confident and mindful driver you need to dispel those negative thoughts and focus on positive, confidence-boosting thoughts. Below you will find a collection of tips to help you boost your confidence as a driver.

Learn to Face Your Fear

If you are fearful of getting behind the wheel of a car, know that you are not alone. Many people who suffer from anxiety feel isolated and set apart from others – if you are able to convince yourself that your anxiety does not make you an outcast, you may have an easier time getting over it. One of the best things you can do to overcome your driving anxiety is to actively face your fears. Get yourself out onto the road as often as possible, even if it is only for a few minutes at a time to drive down to the local gas station and back. The more time you spend behind the wheel, the more confident you will become as a driver.

Drive in Safe, Slow Areas for a While

While you are learning to overcome your driving anxiety you may find it helpful to drive only in slow, safe areas for a little while. Minimizing the number of anxiety triggers you are likely to encounter will help you to build confidence in a safe environment. Practice driving around large parking lots when they are most likely to be empty or take a drive through a local business or industrial district on the weekend when there won't be many people around. When you get some experience behind the wheel without having to worry about potential dangers, you will be more prepared to face the road in more challenging situations.

Do Not Add to Your Anxiety

Drive in a way that does not add to your anxiety as much as possible. For example, maintain the speed limit and stay in the slow lane while you are driving on the highway to reduce any anxiety related to driving fast. Always check your mirrors and your blind spots before merging and use your turn signal before turning. Driving as safely as possible will help to reduce the anxiety you feel while driving which will help you to boost your driving confidence as well.

Practice Driving Unfamiliar Routes

For many people, driving anxiety is triggered by feelings of unfamiliarity or a fear of getting lost. If you have mild driving anxiety you may be fine making your commute to work or school but you become anxious when you have to go somewhere you have never been before. Rather than asking someone else to drive on long trips or carpooling when you have to go somewhere you aren't familiar, think of it as an opportunity to improve your driving skills. Planning your route in advance can help you to feel more confident when you hit the road and you can always ask a friend to come with you as backup in case you lose your way or start to feel anxious.

Learn How to Handle Aggressive Drivers

There will always be that one driver on the road who is in a hurry to get somewhere. They drive twenty miles over the speed limit and weave in and out of lanes, honking at anyone who doesn't go their speed. Do not let aggressive drivers like that get to you, and do not take their behavior personally if they honk at you. It doesn't hurt to think about your own actions, to question whether perhaps you forgot to use your turn signal or you were too hesitant in merging to another lane, but do not assign blame to yourself unnecessarily. Drive safely and do what is comfortable for you – don't let aggressive or bad drivers get to you.

Practice Driving in Sub-Par Conditions

For many people with driving anxiety, fear is triggered by certain driving conditions such as night driving or stormy weather. In some cases you may be able to avoid driving in these conditions, but then what happens when they come upon you unexpectedly and you are not prepared to handle them? To make yourself a more confident driver, and to help reduce your driving anxiety, it is a good idea to practice driving in sub-par conditions. When driving at night, make sure to keep your speed steady and focus on the left-hand curb to maintain proper position in your lane. Avoid looking at headlights and maintain a safe speed as you drive. When driving in the rain, drive only as fast as you feel comfortable and keep to the slow lane when driving on the highway. Avoid braking suddenly and always use your turn signal because stormy conditions may make it hard for other drivers to see you.

Test Yourself with Parking Challenges

Parking is another anxiety-inducing event for many people who suffer from driving anxiety. Not only can parking in a crowded lot or on a busy street be nerve-wracking, but it becomes especially challenging when other drivers are waiting on you. Rather than worrying about other drivers judging your performance, focus on your technique and safety. It is also a good idea to practice different parking challenges at a time when you will not be rushed. Go to an empty parking lot or parking garage and practice pulling into and out of various spaces – you can even set up cones outside your house to practice parallel parking. The more you practice different types of parking challenges, the better and more confident you will become. By practicing without rushing, your skills will be improved for the times when you actually have people waiting on you.

Learn How to Handle Back-Seat Drivers

Having someone criticize your driving can be anxiety-inducing, even for those who typically don't suffer from driving anxiety. It can be good to have another person in the car sometimes, especially if you are nervous about driving alone, but do not let that other person make you question your driving ability or shake your confidence. People who are critical of another's driving often think they are being helpful when, in reality, they are only causing the other person to become anxious. If someone is being critical of your driving, do not be afraid to tell them that their negative comments are distracting or stressful – if they are unwilling to change, you may need to avoid driving with them in the future. Sometimes, having the radio on can help to discourage conversation or criticism, as long as it doesn't distract you while driving.

3.) Take Control of Your Fear

Reducing your driving anxiety is about taking control of your fear rather than letting it control you. You have already learned a great deal about anxiety and have received plenty of useful tips for reducing your anxiety, but there is still more for you to learn. Aside from facing your fears, practicing your driving skills, and engaging in mindfulness techniques there are other things you can do to keep your anxiety at bay. Some things you might consider trying include:

- Improving your diet
- Reducing your caffeine intake
- Managing your daily stress levels
- Avoiding anticipatory anxiety
- Engaging in positive affirmation
- Desensitizing yourself to your anxiety

a.) Improving Your Diet

You may not realize it, but the foods you put into your body have a direct impact on your health and wellbeing – they can also affect your anxiety. Studies have shown that there are certain foods that can help you to feel more calm and relaxed while other foods may exacerbate the symptoms of anxiety. Some of the foods that may help to reduce anxiety include:

- **Turkey** – Turkey is rich in an amino acid called tryptophan which helps to relieve stress and increase serotonin production.

- **Beef** – This food is rich in Vitamin B which helps to improve mood and ward off anxiety – Vitamin B deficiencies have been linked to depression in some people.

- **Whole Wheat Bread** – Whole grains can help to increase serotonin production in the brain which may lift your mood and relieve anxiety. Whole grains are absorbed more slowly by the body so you don't get the sudden blood sugar spikes you get with processed grains and sugars.

- **Salmon** – Salmon is rich in omega-3 fatty acids like EPA and DHA which not only reduce your risk for heart disease but can lift your mood as well.

- **Greek Yogurt** – High-protein foods like Greek yogurt help to stimulate production of dopamine and norepinephrine in the brain which improves your alertness and your mood.

- **Turmeric** – Foods seasoned with turmeric are rich in an antioxidant called curcumin which help to enhance mood and relieve depression, a condition commonly linked to anxiety disorders.

- **Avocado** – Avocadoes are not only rich in monounsaturated fats which support brain health and neurotransmitter production but they also contain potassium which helps to lower blood pressure.

- **Dark Chocolate**–Dark chocolate, when eaten in moderation, has been shown to provide a number of significant health benefits. In one trial it was discovered that individuals who consumed 1.5 ounces of dark chocolate per day felt significantly calmer than those who did not.

- **Asparagus** – This vegetable is rich in sulfur and folic acid, a B vitamin – one 5.3-ounce serving of asparagus provides nearly 60% of your daily recommended value for folic acid.

- **Leafy Greens** – Leafy greens like spinach and Swiss chard are rich in magnesium, a vitamin which helps to regulate your brain-adrenal axis and which helps you to feel calm.

Not only are there certain foods which help to reduce anxiety, but some foods exacerbate the symptoms of anxiety disorders. Some of these foods have a stimulatory effect on the body while others may interfere with the production of certain neurotransmitters in the brain like serotonin or norepinephrine. Some foods that may contribute to anxiety could include:

- Coffee, other caffeinated drinks
- Sugary foods, even artificial sweeteners
- Alcohol and beer (alcohol is a depressant)
- Processed foods (linked to depression)

To truly take control of your anxiety, you can make simple changes to your diet. Try to avoid processed foods, fast foods, and fried foods in favor of fresh, wholesome foods. Eat as many fresh fruits and vegetables as you can along with lean proteins, healthy fats, and whole grains. Limit your intake of alcohol and caffeinated drinks and be sure to drink plenty of water. Pay attention to any food allergies or sensitivities you may have because these could also contribute to anxiety.

b.) Reducing Your Caffeine Intake

As you have already learned in previous chapters, anxiety is closely linked to stress and chronic stress can impact your quality of sleep. When you wake feeling unrested, it can be tempting to reach for a large mug of coffee and to keep refilling that mug all day long. Drinking too much coffee can make you feel jittery and it may also contribute to feelings of anxiety since you are already worked up. Coffee and other caffeinated drinks may not cause anxiety, but they can contribute to it.

There have been a number of studies conducted regarding the relationship between caffeine and anxiety. For those with mild anxiety (not an anxiety disorder), moderate amounts of caffeine may actually be helpful. It was also found, however, that those with daily anxiety did not need as much coffee to experience the same effects as those without anxiety. Given this information, you can see how drinking too much coffee could have a negative impact on your anxiety.

Caffeine has been linked to panic attacks in particular, especially since the effects of caffeine are similar to the symptoms of a panic attack – increased heart rate and increased energy. If you suffer from severe anxiety and panic attacks, drinking caffeinated beverages could trigger a panic attack by causing the symptoms you have learned to identify with a panic attack. When you start to feel your heart beating faster and you feel a rush of energy flowing through your system, your anxiety might kick in and amplify those symptoms, leading to a panic attack. You do not necessarily need to give up coffee and other caffeinated beverages completely, but you should become aware of how these beverages affect your anxiety and consume them in moderation accordingly.

c.) Managing Daily Stress Levels

Everyone experiences stress at some time or another but people with anxiety have a particularly acute reaction to stress. Stress is a response to a threat in a specific situation, but anxiety is a reaction to that stress. The more stressed you are, the more anxious you become as a result of that stress. Chronic stress can also lead to physical symptoms like headache, heart palpitations, chest pain, and insomnia. Some of these symptoms are also linked to anxiety, so if you experience these symptoms as a result of stress, it could trigger your anxiety.

Managing and reducing your daily stress levels can have a seriously beneficial effect on your anxiety. Try engaging in some of the breathing exercises and relaxation techniques provided earlier in this book to reduce your stress.

Improving your diet and making an effort to get more sleep will also help you to reduce your stress levels. Getting a little bit of exercise each day, taking breaks during your work day, and engaging in meditation practices can also be beneficial.

d.) Avoiding Anticipatory Anxiety

Not only do people with anxiety experience fear in certain situations, but they may also become anxious in anticipation of being put in those situations. For example, if you suffer from driving anxiety you may become anxious simply at the thought of driving. Avoid giving in to the temptation to feed this sort of anxiety by indulging in your worries. Rather, acknowledge your fears and worries but do not give in to them. Tell yourself, "Yes, I feel anxious about _____ but I know I can handle it".

e.) Engaging in Positive Affirmation

Avoiding anticipatory anxiety will help to reduce your anxiety responses in certain situations. Another helpful tool to help reduce your general anxiety is to engage in positive affirmation. People who suffer from anxiety often blame themselves or suffer from low self-esteem. The more you put yourself down, the more anxious you will become. So, to reduce your anxiety, you need to start building yourself back up!

Rather than putting yourself down for being anxious in a certain situation, offer yourself some positive affirmations. Instead of thinking, "I am a terrible driver because I am anxious on the road," think, "I am a careful driver and I take steps to ensure the safety of myself and others while driving". You may find it helpful to write positive affirmations to yourself on post-it notes and to place them

1Chapter Five: Feeling Safe, Confident and Comfortable

on your mirror, refrigerator, and other places around the house where you will see them. Read those affirmations out loud before you go to bed at night and again in the morning. This may sound silly at first, but you will be amazed at the positive effects it can have.

f.) Desensitizing Yourself to Your Anxiety

If your fear of driving become debilitating, it may be more difficult for you to overcome it than it is for lesser levels of anxiety. One therapeutic technique that may be particularly useful for you is desensitization. Desensitization is a process through which you fact your fears in small steps, reconditioning yourself from having a fearful or negative response to having no response or a positive response instead. For example, if you are incredibly anxious about driving a car you might start off by spending some time sitting in the car without driving it to desensitize yourself to the experience. You will learn more about desensitization techniques in the next chapter.

The Mindful Driver   P a g e | 78

Chapter Six: Desensitization Technique Overcome Anxiety

In this chapter you will learn the basics about what desensitization is and how it can be applied to anxiety. Desensitization can be an incredibly effective tool for re-conditioning your brain against producing a fear response in certain situations and it is highly effective in treating driving anxiety. In this chapter you will receive step-by-step guides for practicing systematic desensitization and for applying those techniques to your driving anxiety.

1.) What is Desensitization and How Can it Help?

Many people who suffer from anxiety become conditioned to react to certain situations in a particular way. For example, someone with driving anxiety may produce a fear response when driving a car, even if there is no present danger. This is not something that you did on purpose, or even something that you can help from happening, but there is something you can do to counteract it – desensitization exercises. Desensitization is the process of gradually exposing yourself to your fears in incremental amounts so that you become less sensitive to them. In essence, you will be re-conditioning your body to stop the fear response from happening.

One of the most effective methods of desensitization for anxiety-related problems is called systematic desensitization. To utilize this process you imagine the events that cause your anxiety and then engage in a relaxation exercise to dissipate the anxiety you feel. With repetition you will eventually come to find that your anxiety response to the imagined event becomes less severe. That way, when you face the event for real, you will be much less anxious.

To help you gain an understanding of what desensitization is and how it works. The systematic desensitization process has three steps:

1. Relaxation
2. Constructing an anxiety hierarchy
3. Pairing relaxation with the anxiety hierarchy

1.) Relaxation

In this first step you should engage in some kind of relaxation exercise to put yourself into a deeply relaxed state of mind. You can choose whatever relaxation technique you like, as long as it works for you.

2.) Constructing an Anxiety Hierarchy

In this step you will construct imaginary versions of certain situations and scenes involving your primary fear. Some of these situations may be things you have actually experienced while others will be made-up. For example, if you have a fear of flying your anxiety hierarchy may contain things like standing in the ticket line, checking your bags, boarding the flight, taking off, experiencing turbulence in the air, and making an emergency landing.

Once you have about 10 to 15 scenes or situations in mind you can write them out on index cards and sort them into different categories according to the level of anxiety each situation would produce. Use the following scale to rate your anxiety hierarchy items:

Low Anxiety (1 to 19)

Medium-Low Anxiety (20 to 39)

Moderate Anxiety (40 to 59)

Medium-High Anxiety (60 to 79)

High Anxiety (80 to 100)

As you organize and sort your anxiety scenes, try to include at least two items in each anxiety level. Once you have completed your organization, place all of the cards in a pile organized from low anxiety to high anxiety.

3.) Paring Relaxation with the Anxiety Hierarchy – After you've created your anxiety hierarchy, you then need to start pairing your relaxation techniques with the scenes and situations on the index cards. You should already be familiar with your relaxation technique and should have practiced it several times. The goal for this third step is to desensitize yourself to no more than three or your anxiety hierarchy items in each session, and each session should last no more than 30 minutes. During each session you should begin with the last item you worked with during your previous session. Follow the steps below to use the systematic desensitization procedure:

1. Use your preferred relaxation technique to put your mind and body in a deep state of relaxation.

2. Read the index card for the first item in your anxiety hierarchy.

3. Imagine yourself in that situation for a few seconds, picturing it in as much detail as possible (you should begin with a few seconds the first time and increase the duration with each repetition).

4. Stop imagining the situation and assess your level of anxiety – rate yourself on a scale from 0 to 100.

5. Re-establish your level of deep relaxation and rest for about 30 seconds before continuing.

6. Re-read the index card and imagine yourself in that situation for a tolerable amount of time – re-evaluate your level of anxiety.

7. If you are still experiencing a measurable amount of anxiety, return to Step 2 – if you are not feeling anxious, move on to the next item in your hierarchy.

8. Repeat this process with no more than three of your index cards then end your session with a period of 3 to 5 minutes of deep relaxation.

While engaging in this type of desensitization procedure, you may encounter problems. If you do not experience any anxiety upon reading the index cards, it may because you have not imagined the situation vividly enough. Try imagining the situation in greater detail or focus on it for a longer period of time. If you find that a certain item produces a consistent level of anxiety that does not decrease with repetition, it may be because the scene is too detailed or that it contains elements from scenes later in your hierarchy. Try rewriting the description or rearrange your hierarchy more accurately.

2.) Step-by-Step Guide for Desensitization

Now that you are familiar with the idea of desensitization and understand the procedure involved you are ready to learn how to apply this method to your driving anxiety. Below you will find a step-by-step guide for desensitizing yourself to driving anxiety:

1. Establish a particularly relaxation technique that works for you and engage in this practice for several

minutes until you feel deeply relaxed.

2. Walk out to your car and sit in the driver's seat with the engine off for 10 to 30 seconds.

3. Exit the vehicle and go inside – once inside, assess your level of anxiety.

4. If you are feeling symptoms of anxiety, take a few deep breaths until you feel relaxed again and then go back out to the car and sit in the driver's seat for another 20 to 30 seconds.

5. Go back inside and re-evaluate your level of anxiety – if you are still feeling anxious, repeat Step 4. If you are not feeling anxious, move on to the next step.

6. Walk out to your car, sit in the driver's seat and turn the engine on – sit in the car for 10 to 30 seconds.

7. Exit the vehicle and go inside – once inside, assess your level of anxiety. If you are feeling symptoms of anxiety, take a few deep breaths until you feel relaxed again and then repeat Step 6.

8. If you are not feeling anxious, put the car in Drive and drive your vehicle a few yards up the road – pull over to the side of the road, put the car in park, and turn off the engine.

9. Assess your level of anxiety – if you are feeling anxious, take a few deep breaths until you feel calm again.

10. Drive the car forward again, a little further than the last time, then pull over and assess your level of anxiety. If you are feeling anxious, take a few deep breaths to relax yourself – if you are not feeling anxious, drive around the block and pull back into your driveway.

This is as far as you should go during your first desensitization session. You do not want to push yourself too far the first time or you might be too anxious to pick it up again later. Really focus on relaxing yourself before you begin and pay close attention to your level of anxiety as you execute each step. Do not move on to the next level until you are confident that you are feeling no anxiety. You may need to repeat this entire session several times over the course of a week before you are ready to move on. Once you are able to drive your car around the block without anxiety you can move on to the next session.

When you are ready to move on, follow the steps below:

1. Engage in your relaxation technique until you are fully relaxed before you get in your car.

2. Walk out to your car then sit in the driver's seat and turn the keys in the ignition. Put the car in gear and drive down the road.

3. Drive a little further down the road then you did during the first session – try to drive with a destination in mind like a nearby gas station.

4. Assess your level of anxiety – if you are feeling anxious, take a few deep breaths until you feel calm again.

5. Drive back to your house and park in the driveway – turn off the car and assess your level of anxiety. If you are feeling anxious, take a few deep breaths and then make the same trip again until you do not feel anxious when you arrive.

6. Once you have conquered your anxiety for longer trips you can test yourself by driving on a highway – try to drive at a time when there will not be a great deal of traffic.

7. Drive on the highway for a few miles as long as you are able to do so safely without extreme anxiety then exit the highway and park your car somewhere safe.

8. Assess your level of anxiety – if you are feeling anxious, take a few deep breaths until you feel calm

again.

9. Once you have calmed down, get back on the highway and drive for another few miles before exiting and assessing your level of anxiety.

10. You can repeat this sequence two or three times before you head back home – when you get home, sit in the car and take deep breaths until you are fully relaxed before going back into the house.

Keep using this technique to test yourself in different situations. Once you are able to drive for a few miles on the highway without anxiety you can try doing it at a time when there is likely to be more traffic. Test yourself with longer drives each time and try to introduce challenges like driving at night, driving in the rain, driving to an unfamiliar location, or parking along a busy street. The more situations you can think of to test yourself in, the less anxious you will become each time you get in the car. It is all about practice and relaxation – do not move on to the next step until you are able to do so without anxiety and relax yourself before you start.

Chapter Seven: Meditation in Motion

When you hear the word "meditation," what do you think of? You probably picture someone sitting cross-legged on the ground with their palms on their knees, chanting something in a low, rhythmic way. In reality, meditation means many things – it can mean something as simple as practicing breathing exercises and it is something you can even do while driving. Practicing meditation while driving can help you feel more at ease on the road. In this chapter you will learn about meditation in general as well as some tips for meditating while driving.

1.) Addressing Misconceptions About Meditation

Before getting into the details of what meditation is, you might find it helpful to learn what meditation it not. Below you will find an overview of some of the most common misconceptions about meditation:

1. Meditation is about relaxation and nothing more.

While relaxation is one of the main benefits of meditation, it is not the only benefit. Regularly practicing meditation can help you to become more self-aware and it may help to promote inner and outer healing. Meditation may also help you to free yourself from destructive though processes and negative emotions.

2. Meditation is something "holy" people practice.

People who do not know much about meditation tend to think that it is only for holy or religious people. In reality, meditation has benefits for everyone. Meditation is simply a practice that involves focused thinking and breathing exercises – anyone can do those things.

3. Meditation takes a long time.

A common misconception about meditation is that it is something you have to do for a long time. You do not necessarily need to spend hours meditating each day to experience the benefits – you can meditate for a few minutes in the morning or right before you get in your car to help relax your body and calm your mind.

4. Meditation is about thinking about nothing.

You have probably heard the phrase "clear your mind" used in the context of meditation, but meditation is not about thinking of nothing. Instead, meditation is about focusing your thoughts to increase your own awareness of yourself and your mind. By focusing your thoughts inward you can calm your anxiety and reduce stress.

5. Meditation involves going into a trance.

Meditation is not hypnosis – you do not need to go into a trance or be put to sleep in order to do it. During meditation, the goal is not to zone out from reality but to focus your thoughts inward and to process your thoughts and emotions more fully.

2.) The Basics of Meditation

Meditation is an important aspect of Traditional Chinese Medicine (TCM) which is the type of medicine practiced in ancient China thousands of years ago. While TCM originated thousands of years ago, it is still practiced in many areas today as part of Eastern medicine. Traditional Chinese Medicine incorporates a number of different practices including meditation, acupuncture, herbal medicine, tai chi, and qigong.

Many TCM practices are founded on the idea of *qi*. *Qi* is the vital energy that flows through and around the body. It travels throughout the body along specific paths, called meridians, which are connected to specific elements, organs, senses, and emotions. The key idea behind Traditional Chinese Medicine is that health problems and disease are caused by disruptions in the flow of or imbalances of *qi* and that correct those imbalances is the best way to treat the problem.

Another idea that plays a key role in Traditional Chinese Medicine is the idea of harmony. When your qi flows smoothly throughout the body, your body is said to be in harmony. One of the best ways to foster harmony in the body, and between the mind and body, is through meditation. The TCM practice of qigong involves various mind and body exercises designed to improve the circulation of *qi* through the body for the purpose of cleansing or healing. Below you will find a step-by-step guide for a basic qigong breathing exercise:

1. Sit comfortably on the edge of a straight-backed chair – your back should not be against the chair.

2. Bend your knees and gently rest your palms on your knees, keeping your arms loose.

3. Close your eyes and rest the tip of the tongue against the roof of your mouth, just behind your teeth (as if you were making a "le" sound).

4. Breathe in through your nose, filling your belly with air and expanding your lungs.

5. Exhale slowly through your mouth, breathing out a little bit more than you inhaled – do not puff out your chest as you exhale.

6. Keep breathing, inhaling to only about 70% of your lung capacity to keep your body from becoming tense and to promote relaxation.

Practicing this basic qigong meditation technique in the morning when you wake and again before bed time may help to reduce your anxiety by promoting general relaxation. Qigong has been linked to a number of health benefits including reduced stress levels, increased vitality, improved immune function, increased harmony and balance, and relief from chronic disease symptoms. In the next section you will learn how to meditate while driving.

3.) Practicing Meditation While Driving

Performing meditation exercises (like the qigong breathing exercise from the previous chapter) before you get into your car may help you to feel more relaxed and less anxious. For many people, however, that is only half the battle – you also need something to keep you from becoming anxious while you drive. While you should not close your eyes while driving, there are certain aspects of meditation techniques that you can practice safely while you drive to combat driving anxiety.

As you drive, try to sit up straight and maintain the natural curve of your spine – you may find it helpful to put the seat in the upright position and place a small pillow at the base of your spine. While driving you should try to keep your body as relaxed as possible and avoid fidgeting – do not tap your fingers on the steering wheel or shake your leg. These actions will only fuel your anxiety, so you need to try to keep as still as possible, making only the necessary movements to turn the wheel, pump the brakes, and check your mirrors.

In addition to maintaining a straight but relaxed posture, you should also cultivate an environment of relaxation in your vehicle. Turn off the radio and put your phone on silent so it does not disturb you – these things will help to promote relaxation while also improving your focus while driving. Once you have eliminated these distractions and gotten into a relaxed but upright posture you can begin your meditation exercise. Follow the steps below to meditate while driving:

1. Open your eyes to everything going on around you – pay attention to other cars and drivers as well as the

environment beyond the road.

2. Listen carefully to the sounds of your vehicle on the road and the sounds of traffic around you.

3. Pay attention to the physical sensations you are experiencing – the feeling of the wheel under your fingers and the seat beneath your body.

4. As you become aware of the sights, sounds, and sensations of driving you will become more focused on your experience and less focused on your anxiety.

5. Allow yourself to see, hear, and feel everything as you drive and avoid letting your mind wander toward other things – this will help you foster a feeling of tranquility.

6. As you drive, try incorporating the breathing technique from the previous section.

7. Take long, deep breaths in through your nose, letting the air fill your belly.

8. Exhale slowly through your mouth without puffing out your chest – let your bell return to normal.

9. Repeat this breathing pattern until it becomes something you do without thinking about it – keep focusing on the sights, sounds, and sensations of driving.

10. If it helps you to feel calm and focused you can also try humming or vocally repeating a relaxing phrase to yourself as you drive.

Meditation techniques are easy to customize, so find a rhythm and a breathing pattern that works for you. The more frequently you use meditation techniques while driving the more second-nature it will become. Before long you will find yourself relaxed and focused while driving without even having to think about your breathing techniques.

Chapter Eight: General Mindfulness Exercises

At this point in the book you have learned a great deal about anxiety in general and driving anxiety in particular. Not only have you learned the basics about this overwhelming condition, you have received a variety of specific tips for dealing with your driving anxiety and hopefully for reducing it. Remember though, this is only an introduction –the beginning of a gradual process of positive change. I would advise exploring your chosen technique in depth, consider attending mindfulness classes, either online or in person – as Mindfulness becomes increasingly popular an increasing amount of easily accessible resources are becoming available - why not challenge yourself and find a local class? Join yoga, take small mindful drives around your local neighborhood and begin to enjoy sitting behind the wheel once more. To end this book, I would like to leave you with some important things to remember about your anxiety as well as some general mindfulness techniques. You will find both in the upcoming pages of this chapter.

1.) Your Anxiety is Not Your Fault

One of the most important things I want you to draw from this book is the idea that your anxiety is not your fault. Many people who suffer from anxiety, particularly driving anxiety, feel weak or stupid but I want you to understand that your anxiety does not define who you are. It may be a challenge that you have to deal with, but having anxiety doesn't make you a bad person or a weak person. In fact, it makes you an incredibly strong and determined person if you make an effort to face your fears and to deal with your anxiety rather than letting it control you.

I used to be in your shoes – afraid to get behind the wheel or to even think about driving my car. I couldn't even drive to the grocery store or take my daughter to ballet class without feeling a crushing weight on my chest at the thought of getting in the car. I knew my fears were irrational, but I was powerless to stop them – I had become conditioned to fear the thought of driving and my fear response was completely automatic. Even though I knew there was nothing to be afraid of, I could not stop my anxiety from creeping up on me.

It wasn't until I began to do some research on my own that I came to understand my anxiety. What I discovered is that my fear of driving had created pathways in my brain that my neurons became used to following. Think of your brain like an old LP record with grooves that the record player needle followed to play the music – the only way the record player would work is if you put the needle in that groove. Over time, the groove got deeper and deeper until it became so worn out that you had to replace the record entirely.

My driving anxiety was just like that old, worn-out record. At some point I had become fixated on the idea that driving was dangerous and the more I repeated that idea in my brain, the more engrained it became. My brain formed a pathway so that each time I thought about driving, it triggered an automatic fear response and each time I experienced that fear, the groove got a little bit deeper. I was a victim of my brain, suffering as a result of a conditioned response that I had no intention of creating. My brain had tricked me and I was determined to re-condition myself and to overcome my anxiety.

Through a combination of research and talk therapy, I came to form a deeper understanding of my anxiety. I was able to identify a handle of triggers and worked hard to desensitize myself to those triggers. I used many of the same techniques I have written about in this book, so I can assure you that these things truly work! If you are willing to put in the time and effort, you can take control of your fears and fight back against your anxiety. Your driving anxiety does not have to become a crushing fear that keeps you from leaving the house. It will take time, but you have it in you to take back control of your life!

2.) Tips for General Mindfulness

Though you've already received some detailed tips for mindful driving, I would like to leave you with a few additional tips for general mindfulness. You can use these tips to increase your general mindfulness as a means of dealing with everyday anxiety. Apply these mindfulness tips to your individual struggles and you may be surprised to see what kind of change you can create.

- Be conscious of your breathing – take a few moments out of your day to just focus on the feeling of breath coming into and out of your lungs.

- With each task you perform, become in-tune with your senses – when you are eating, focus on the taste and texture of your food. When you are washing dishes, focus on the feeling of the warm water and the slippery soap. When you take a walk outside, notice the feeling of the sun on your skin and the breeze in your hair.

- Take a few moments each day to simply be – do not try to fill every moment of every day with activity. For just a few minutes each day, let yourself become completely relaxed and focused on yourself.

- Realize that your thoughts are not always true and you do not need to give them the power to harm you – learn to recognize destructive thoughts and stop them before they become engrained in your mind.

- Start to recognize the areas of your life where you tend to go on autopilot – it may be when surfing the web, while doing the dishes, or when getting ready for bed. Make an effort to become more aware during those moments and more mindful of your activities.

- Practice listening to others without making judgments on them – simply listen to and accept their thoughts and opinions. This will help you to do the same for yourself.

Hopefully, in putting some of these mindfulness techniques into place, you will increase your awareness of yourself and of your thoughts. Mindfulness is about living in the moment and increasing your awareness. If you practice these mindfulness techniques regularly, your anxiety will reduce – there's nothing surer.

Conclusion

After reading this book, it is my hope that you have a deeper and more thorough understanding of yourself and your anxiety. I hope that you have learned that you are not alone in your anxiety – anxiety is completely normal and it is something that countless individuals are forced to deal with on a daily basis. Anxiety can be debilitating for many people, but it is my hope that you believe that it does not have to be – you can learn to deal with and to overcome your anxiety, especially when it comes to driving.

By following the tips in this book you will be able to face your fears, reduce your anxiety, and become comfortable and confident on the road. Overcoming your anxiety is not something that you can do overnight but, with a little time and effort, it is entirely possible. By utilizing the steps outlined in this book you will be able to take control of your fears and to take back your life from your anxiety – you will learn to be a mindful driver, for your own safety and the safety of others, so that you can face the open road with confidence.

Enjoy.

Index

C

D

E

F

G

H

I

P

Q

R

S

References

"10 Tips to Start Being Mindful Now." Mindful.org.
<http://www.mindful.org/mindfulness-practice/10-tips-for-being-mindful-right-now>

"13 Foods to Help Ease Anxiety and Stress." Mind Body
Green. <http://www.mindbodygreen.com/0-15428/13-foods-to-help-ease-anxiety-stress.html>

"Anxiety and the Brain: An Introduction." Calm Clinic.
<http://www.calmclinic.com/anxiety/anxiety-brain>

"Applying Mindfulness to Driving." Headspace Daily.
<https://www.headspace.com/blog/view/221/applying-mindfulness-to-driving>

"Breathing: Three Exercises." Dr. Weil.
<http://www.drweil.com/drw/u/ART00521/three-breathing-exercises.html>

Christensen, James. "How to Overcome Fear of Driving –
Five Easy Ways to Conquer Your Fear."

"Coping with Anxiety: Can Diet Make a Difference?" Mayo Clinic. <http://www.mindbodygreen.com/0-15428/13-foods-to-help-ease-anxiety-stress.html>

"Does Coffee Cause Anxiety?" Calm Clinic. <http://www.calmclinic.com/anxiety/causes/coffee>

"Driving Anxiety and Panic Attacks While Driving." MD Junction. <http://www.mdjunction.com/forums/panic-attacks-discussions/general-support/2538964-driving-anxiety-and-panic-attacks-while-driving>

"How Meditation Helps with Difficult Emotions." Mindful.com. <http://www.mindful.org/mindful-magazine/glimpse-getting-started-2>

"How to Be a Confident Driver." All About You. <http://www.allaboutyou.com/country/travel-advice/better-driving-driving-fear>

"How to Reduce Anxiety While Driving." Calm Clinic. <http://www.calmclinic.com/anxiety/types/driving>

"Meditation in Motion." Depth & Liberation. Adam Coutts. <http://www.intromeditation.com/Wordpress/meditation-while-driving/>

"Mindfulness Exercises: Mindful Driving." About Health. <http://bpd.about.com/od/livingwithbpd/a/minddriving.htm>

Moreno, Ted. "How to Deal with Driving Anxiety." Hypnosis Motivation Institute. <https://hypnosis.edu/articles/driving-anxiety>

"Overcoming Driving Phobia." Anxiety Care UK. <http://www.anxietycare.org.uk/docs/driving.asp>

"Preparation and Posture Guide." Fragrant Heart. <http://www.fragrantheart.com/cms/preparation-and-posture>

Salters-Pedneault, Kristalyn. "Mindfulness Exercises: Mindful Driving." About Health. <http://bpd.about.com/od/livingwithbpd/a/minddriving.htm>

"Street Stress: tips to Reduce Anxiety While Driving." Mood Radiance. <http://www.moodradiance.com/reduce-anxiety-while-driving/>

"Symptoms." Anxiety and Depression Association of
    America. <http://www.adaa.org/understanding-
    anxiety/panic-disorder-agoraphobia/symptoms>

"Systematic Desensitization." A Guide to Psychology and
    its Practice. <http://www.guidetopsychology.com/
    sysden.htm>

Weber, Greg. "Do You Have Anxiety Driving on
    Highways?" Driving Peace.
    <http://www.drivingpeace.com/do-you-have-anxiety-
    driving-on-highways/#.VWyCaM9VhBc>

"What Anxiety Does to Your Brain and What You Can Do
    About It." Dr. Mercola. <http://articles.mercola.com/
    sites/articles/archive/2013/12/05/anxiety.aspx>

"What is Anxiety?" Anxiety BC.
    <http://www.anxietybc.com/resources/anxiety.php>

"What is Mindfulness?" Greater Good.
    <http://greatergood.berkeley.edu/topic/mindfulness/defi
    nition>

CPSIA information can be obtained
at www.ICGtesting.com
Printed in the USA
FSHW021256271021
85782FS

9 780993 168345